5-13-01

To the most wonderful
Mom who is always
there no matter what.
Thank you.
            Love
            Susie

Mother...

There are so many words
I could try to say to you
to let you know
how much you mean to me,
but really
the two most important feelings
I want you to know are...

"Thank you"
for all your love,
and
"I love you"
with all my heart.

Deanna Beisser

Other books in the *"Language of"* Series...

Blue Mountain Arts®

The Language of Courage and Inner Strength

The Language of Friendship

The Language of Happiness

The Language of Love

The Language of Marriage

The Language of Positive Thinking

The Language of Prayer

The Language of Recovery

The Language of Success

The Language of Teaching

The Language of Teenagers

Thoughts to Share with a Wonderful Father

Thoughts to Share with a Wonderful Son

Thoughts to Share with a Wonderful Daughter

It's Great to Have a Brother like You

It's Great to Have a Sister like You

The "Language of" Series...

Thoughts to Share with a
WONDERFUL
MOTHER

A Blue Mountain Arts® Collection

Blue Mountain Press ®

SPS Studios, Inc., Boulder, Colorado

Library of Congress Catalog Card Number: 98-46832
ISBN: 0-88396-487-2

ACKNOWLEDGMENTS appear on page 48.

Certain trademarks are used under license.

Manufactured in Thailand
Fourth Printing: April 2000

♻ This book is printed on recycled paper.

Library of Congress Cataloging-in-Publication Data

Thoughts to share with a wonderful mother : a Blue Mountain Arts collection.

    p.   cm.
  ISBN 0-88396-487-2 (alk. paper)
  1. Mothers--Literary collections. 2. Motherhood--Literary
collections. 1. SPS Studios (Firm)
  PN6071.M7 L36 1999
  306.874'3--dc21

                                           98-46832
                                             CIP
                                           Rev.

SPS Studios, Inc.
P.O. Box 4549, Boulder, Colorado 80306

Contents

(Authors listed in order of first appearance)

The Love Between
a Mother and Her Child Is Forever

The love between
a mother and her child
is a bond of the strongest kind.
It is a love of the present,
interwoven with memories
of the past
and dreams of the future.
It is strengthened by
overcoming obstacles and
facing fears and challenges together.
It is having pride in each other
and knowing that our love
can withstand anything.
It is sacrifice and tears,
laughter and hugs.
It is understanding, patience,
and believing in each other.

It is wanting only the best
for each other
and wanting to help anytime
there is a need.
It is respect, a hug,
and unexpected kindness.
It is making time to be together
and knowing just what to do and say.
It is an unconditional,
forever kind of love.

— Barbara Cage

My Mother

For as long as I can remember
you have been by my side
to give me support
to give me confidence
to give me help

For as long as I can remember
you have always been the person
I looked up to
so strong
so sensitive
so pretty

For as long as I can remember
and still today
you are everything a mother should be

For as long as I can remember
you have always provided stability
within our family
full of laughter
full of tears
full of love

So much of what I have become
is because of you
and I want you to know
that I appreciate you, thank you
and love you
more than words can express

Susan Polis Schutz

Mother...

I am proud and thankful
that you are the woman
who raised me.
I'll never forget the love
you have shown me
or your constant support
and encouragement.
You always believe in me,
and that has helped me
to become the person I am.
Our relationship
may seem to have changed
over the years,
but I know our love hasn't.
The bond we share can't be changed;
we are together even when we are apart,
for you are forever in my heart,
and I love you.

Barbara Cage

I search among the plain
and lovely words
To find what the one word
"Mother" means…

"Mother" — a word that holds
the tender spell
Of all the dear essential
things of earth;
A home, clean sunlit rooms,
and the good smell
Of bread; a table spread;
a glowing hearth.
And love beyond
the dream of anyone…
I search for words for her…
and there are none.

Grace Noll Crowell

Mother is the name for God
in the lips and hearts of little children.

William Makepeace Thackeray

Every thing in nature bespeaks the mother. The sun is the mother of the earth and gives it its nourishment of heat; it never leaves the universe at night until it has put the earth to sleep to the song of the sea and the hymn of the birds and brooks. And this earth is the mother of trees and flowers. It produces them, nurses them, and weans them. The trees and flowers become kind mothers of their great fruits and seeds. And the mother, the prototype of all existence, is the eternal spirit, full of beauty and love.

Kahlil Gibran

A mother is the truest friend we have, when trials, heavy and sudden fall upon us; when adversity takes the place of prosperity; when friends who rejoice with us in our sunshine desert us; when trouble thickens around us, still will she cling to us, and endeavor by her kind precepts and counsels to dissipate the clouds of darkness, and cause peace to return to our hearts.

— Washington Irving

The hand that rocks the cradle
    is the hand that rules the world.

— William Ross Wallace

I think my life began with waking up
and loving my mother's face.

George Eliot

In life,
we are lucky if we can find
a best friend whom we can
trust and admire and love.
But when that friend
is also our mother,
then we are twice blessed,
and fortunate beyond our dreams.

Audrey Esar

My Perfect Mother

Your heart is big. Your love is pure. You want the best for me and care about everything I'm going through. You often put my needs above your own and overlook my mistakes. You love me without condition. Whatever I am and whatever I do is okay with you. You accept me... all of me. You're more than I could have ever hoped for in a mother. You're my perfect mother, and I'm so thankful for you.

You're always there: to hear my complaints, to share my joy, to feel my pain, to listen to my latest adventure, to advise me, to cry with me and hope for me and laugh with me, to forgive me when I do something dumb. I've never heard a harsh word from you that wasn't justified. I've never seen selfishness from you... only a mother who gives her love freely, happily, joyfully, and perfectly.

If I looked the world over, I could never find a mother more perfect than you. If I could choose anyone at all for my mom, I'd choose you. I'm so lucky that God put me in your family and gave me you for a mother. After all, I wouldn't be me, without you. You're my perfect mother, and I love you and appreciate you more than I could ever express. I hope and pray that you're happy and that your every dream comes true. I pray for your perfect health and unlimited joy.

Donna Fargo

Dear Mother

You know that nothing
can ever change
what we have always been
and always will be
to each other.

Franklin Delano Roosevelt

I have never met anybody in my
life, I think, who loved his mother as
much as I love you. I don't believe
there ever was anybody who did,
quite so much, and quite in so many
wonderful ways.

Edna St. Vincent Millay

I must tell you how much
I love you; that with each day
I learn to extol your love
and your worth more —
and that when I look back
over my life, I can find nothing
in your treatment of me
that I would alter.

I believe, most beloved mother,
that the improvement of the world
can only arise when mothers
like you are increased
thousands of times
and have more children.

— Louis D. Brandeis

MOTHER

The light, the spell-word of the heart,
    Our guiding star in weal or woe,
Our talisman — our earthly chart —
    That sweetest name that earth can know.

We breathed it first with lisping tongue
    When cradled in her arms we lay;
Fond memories round that name are hung
    That will not, cannot pass away.

We breathed it then, we breathe it still,
    More dear than sister, friend, or brother;
The gentle power, the magic thrill,
    Awakened at the name of *mother*.

                — Fanny J. Crosby

M is for the million things she gave me
O means only that she's growing old
T is for the tears were shed to save me
H is for her heart of purest gold
E is for her eyes, with love-light shining
R means right, and right she'll always be
Put them all together they spell "Mother,"
A word that means the world to me.

Theodore Morse and Howard Johnson

The angels, whispering to one another,
Can find, among their burning terms of love,
None so devotional as that of "Mother."

Edgar Allan Poe

Thinking of home
Thinking of the past
Thinking of tomorrow
Brings me closer to you
You are a special person
who brings lasting joy
into my life

Louise Bradford Lowell

Where thou art, that is home.

Emily Dickinson

If there is happiness in my heart,
   it's because you helped put it there.
If there is a gentleness in my beliefs,
   it's because you showed me how to care.
If there is understanding in my thinking,
   it's because you shared your wisdom.
If there is a rainbow over my shoulder,
   it's because of your outlook and your vision.

If there is a knowledge that I can reach out —
   and I really can make some dreams come true —
   it's because I learned from the best
      teacher of all.
         I learned... from you.

                                   Chris Gallatin

The Mother

She never left the children all alone to get their tea.
At home to put the kettle on she always wished to be.
The time we took a holiday and went to see the Fair,
She talked about the children and kept wishing they were there.
There wasn't any pleasure worth the worrying, she said.
She never seemed contented till she'd tucked them all in bed.
As they were growing older she made this her rigid rule,
To be on hand to greet them when they all came home from school.
She never wanted pleasures that her family couldn't share.
She only wanted pretty things for those she loved to wear,
For her heart was with her children, and when came the time to roam
If she couldn't take them with her, she would rather stay at home.
She liked to get their suppers just to know how they were fed.
She had the notion others wouldn't care what prayers they said.
And still serenely happy and as proud as proud can be,
She likes to put the kettle on when they come home for tea.

Edgar A. Guest

Thanks, Mom

Since I had a mother
whose many interests
kept her excited and occupied

Since I had a mother
who interacted with so many people
that she had a real feeling for the world

Since I had a mother
who always was strong
through any period of suffering

Since I had a mother
who was a complete person
I always had a model
to look up to
and that made it easier
for me to develop into
an independent woman

♡ Susan Polis Schutz

A Mother Is...

...always there with a gentle word,
a warm hug, and a smile.

Jennifer Nelson-Fenwick

...someone who encourages your dreams;
applauds your accomplishments;
understands your mistakes;
and is always, always proud of you.

Anna Marie Edwards

...all the patience and forgiveness
that are needed for support
throughout one's life.

Debra Colin-Cooke

...like a blessed candle
Burning through life's long night:
Quietly useful, simple, gentle, tender,
Always giving light.

Lee Shippey

...one vision that never fades from the soul.

H. H. Birkins

...someone who loves
   and is never afraid to show that love...
a listening ear when no one else cares
   or has time to listen.

Dale Harcombe

...she who can take the place of all others,
but whose place no one else can take.

Cardinal Mermillod

...the illuminary that shines and... may weave into
the life of her children thoughts and feelings, rich,
beautiful, grand and noble.

Anonymous

...Kindness, affection, understanding, love, and home. A
blessing beyond compare. A sweetness. The most precious
tenderness. A mother is an angel who is always there.

Collin McCarty

...your dearest friend, always there
when no one else is around,
always giving of herself,
and giving her all.

Cynthia Smith Medina

My Mother

Who fed me from her gentle breast,
And hushed me in her arms to rest,
And on my cheek sweet kisses pressed?
My Mother.

When sleep forsook my open eye,
Who was it sang sweet lullaby,
And rocked me that I should not cry?
My Mother.

Who sat and watched my infant head,
When sleeping on my cradle bed,
And tears of sweet affection shed?
My Mother.

When pain and sickness made me cry,
Who gazed upon my heavy eye,
And wept for fear that I should die?
My Mother.

Who ran to help me when I fell,
And would some pretty story tell,
Or kiss the place to make it well?
My Mother.

Who taught my infant lips to pray,
And love God's holy book and day,
And walk in wisdom's pleasant way?
My Mother.

And can I ever cease to be
Affectionate and kind to thee,
Who was so very kind to me,
My Mother?

Jane Taylor

What Is a Mother?

What is a mother? Who shall answer this?
A mother is a font and spring of life,
A mother is a forest in whose heart
Lies hid a secret ancient as the hills,
For men to claim and take its wealth away;
And like the forest shall her wealth renew
And give, and give again, that men may live.

— Francis Cardinal Spellman

A Mother's Love

A special kind of love that's always there when you need it to comfort and inspire, yet lets you go your own path. A sharing heart filled with patience and forgiveness that takes your side even when wrong. Nothing can take its place.

Debra Colin-Cooke

The god to whom little boys say their prayers has a face very much like their mother's.

Sir James M. Barrie

Our HOME is the place where I first
learned to love and where I first
learned to share.

Our HOME is the place where there is
a person who always cares.

Even if I am far away, the memory of
our HOME remains close in my heart.

Andrew Harding Allen

The mother's heart
     is the child's schoolroom.

Henry Ward Beecher

A house is built of logs and stone,
Of tiles and posts and piers;
A home is built of loving deeds
That stand a thousand years.

— Victor Hugo

Many make the household
but only one the home.

— James Russell Lowell

Mothers never change, I guess,
In their tender thoughtfulness.
All her gentle long life through
She is bent on nursing you;
An' although you may be grown,
She still claims you for her own,
An' to her you'll always be
Just a youngster at her knee.

— Edgar A. Guest

Children are the anchors that hold a mother to life.

— Sophocles

I long for you with the longings of a child to embrace you — to hold you in my arms. I respect you with all the respect due to a mother. You don't know how I love you. So I shall remain, your loving child.

— Margaret Fleming

You never get over being a child, long as you have a mother to go to.

— Sarah Orne Jewett

Sinusoidal Curve

My mother does yoga in candlelight, shadows dancing across her
skin as her heart beats in time to her soft breaths.
When I was a baby, she danced me to sleep with the feathery tune
of her heart beating through warm breasts.
My mother does not like the curve of her hips or the smooth slope
of her arms.
This worries me, because I have those curves and slopes, too.

My mother worries that she worries too much.
My mother gently coaxes green out of our garden,
even in the twilight,
even in the rain.
She still sneaks kisses with my father next to the refrigerator.
My mother does not like parties, but she goes,
and her laughter chimes in with the clinking of glasses.
She wonders about God, sometimes.

When she lights candles, her fingertips dance in swirling circles
around their flames, and
she guides their smoke to her face, where she inhales their warmth
from her cupped palms.

I do not kiss my mother's cheek, and I look away when we argue
so that I do not see her hold the wet light droplets in her eyes with
the soft undersides of her fingers.
I am afraid of my mother's tears because they look so much like mine.

When I speak, I hear her voice gleaming through my words,
which worries me because I have spent so many years finding my own.
I sometimes feel my mother in my chest when I laugh.
My mother believes in angels.
I do too, sometimes.

Amy Cirincione

Mothers and Daughters
Share a Special Bond of Love

The relationship between
a mother and daughter
is comprised of a very deep
understanding of and support for
each other
It is based on an enormous
amount of emotion and love
There is no other relationship
in the world
where two women are so much
like one

— Susan Polis Schutz

Thou are thy mother's glass, and she in thee
Calls back the lovely April of her prime.

— William Shakespeare

There could never have been in my mother's mind any conflict between her children's happiness and her own; they were to her one and the same.

— Harrison Rhodes

For when you looked into my mother's eyes you knew, as if He had told you, why God sent her into the world — it was to open the minds of all who looked, to beautiful thoughts.

— Sir James M. Barrie

God could not be everywhere, so he created mothers.

— Jewish Proverb

Tribute to a Mother

Faith that withstood the shocks of toil and time;
　　Hope that defied despair;
　　Patience that conquered care;
And loyalty, whose courage was sublime;
The great deep heart that was a home for all —
　　Just, eloquent, and strong
　　In protest against wrong;
Wide charity, that knew no sin, no fall;
The Spartan spirit that made life so grand,
　　Mating poor daily needs
　　With high, heroic deeds,
That wrested happiness from Fate's hard hand.

　　　　　　　　　　Louisa May Alcott

Youth fades; love droops,
　　the leaves of friendship fall;
A mother's secret hope
　　outlives them all.

　　　　　　　Oliver Wendell Holmes

A mother's heart is always with her children.

— German Proverb

A mother understands what a child does not say.

— Jewish Proverb

Mother's love is ever in its spring.

— French Saying

A mother's love is best of all.

— West African Proverb

Only One Mother

Most of all the other beautiful things in life
come by twos and threes, by dozens and hundreds.
Plenty of roses, stars, sunsets, rainbows, brothers
and sisters, aunts and cousins, but only one mother
in the whole world.

Kate Douglas Wiggin

Who is it that loves me and will love me
forever with an affection which no chance,
no misery, no crime of mine can do away? —
It is you, my mother.

Thomas Carlyle

When God thought of mother,
He must have laughed with satisfaction,
and framed it quickly —
so rich, so deep, so divine,
so full of soul, power, and beauty,
was the conception.

Henry Ward Beecher

A Mother's Love
Is Never-Ending

A mother's love cannot be compared,
for hers is an ever-constant love,
unlimited, unchanging, and forever.
A mother will hold you while you cry,
soothe you with kind words
when it seems the rest of the world
has turned against you.
A mother will love you when you think
it's impossible that anyone could;
no matter what you have done or said
or failed to do or say,
a mother truly forgives.
A mother will lift your spirits
when you feel there is no hope,
give you confidence and strength
to begin again, and make you laugh
when you think you'll never smile again.
A mother will stand by your side
even when she stands alone;
she will take you as you are,
and never ask for more
than your love in return.

Flo Fessler

Mother

My love for you
is deep and unalterable.
In me, the memory
of your goodness and devotion
will never fade.
I should like to find words
to prove to you
how much I love you,
how my heart is filled
to overflowing with reverence
and gratitude
to you.

— Franz Liszt

I occupy myself... still enveloped in thoughts
of my dear Mother, the most perfect and
magnetic character, the rarest combination of
practical, moral and spiritual, and the least
selfish, of all and any I have ever known —
and by me O so much the most deeply loved.

Walt Whitman

When I think of your loving face,
and of how pleasant it is
to live with you,
of your deep serenity,
your charming tranquility,
I know very well that
I shall never love anyone
as much as you.

— Gustave Flaubert

Oh, the love of a mother,
love which none can forget.

— Victor Hugo

Mother, Your Love Will Live Forever Within Me

You gave me life, nurtured and cared for me, and when you felt the time was right, you set me free. Through the years, never once did you complain or wish for things to be any different. You simply took your life in stride, no questions asked, embracing the happy moments along with the sad, accepting all things for what they were. That was your way.

I didn't always understand or appreciate everything you did. I was a child with my own innocent perception of the world. Now, as a grown-up, I can reflect with such admiration and respect on the wonderful woman and mother you were then and still are today.

You stood with courage to meet the responsibilities that fell upon you, and sacrificed so much for the love of your children. What you have accomplished is more than you will ever realize. When I think of all that you have done for our family and all the love you have so generously poured from your heart, I feel humbled. There will never be enough gratitude to offer to you or a means to repay you. But my heart will always be filled with the joy of knowing your love. It is the most precious gift I have ever received, for it is the one you have so wisely taught me to set free and share with others.

I love you for being a caring person, a remarkable woman, and an exceptional mother. This love that you have given will forever live within me.

debbie peddle

How do you thank someone who has given you the moon and the stars? How do you explain the deepest feelings of the heart? What could you say when the words don't even begin to convey the gratitude? With so much to express, where do you start?

I could spend a lifetime searching for the right words to say to you. The perfect words would be filled with appreciation for someone who took me by the hand when I was little and who guided me on a pathway toward more happiness than most people will ever know.

The right words would tell you how dear you will always be to me for holding the ladders that reached to my own little stars, for catching me whenever I fell, and for always being there with encouragement, support, and understanding.

Maybe I'll never be able to find those perfect words, but that won't keep me from trying. All my life through, I'll try to express that sweet thanks with each little reminder and every big hug —

because you give my heart so much joy
and you give my life so much love.

— Laurel Atherton

Thank You, Mother

Thank you for the sacrifices you have made for me. Thank you for all you've given me and all you've done for me.

I know there have been times that, had it not been for your unselfishness, my life would have been different: not as balanced, not as happy.

Thank you for giving me life. Thank you for your example. Thank you for being my mother. I wouldn't trade you even if I could. I love you so much.

Donna Fargo

ACKNOWLEDGMENTS

We gratefully acknowledge the permission granted by the following authors, publishers, and authors' representatives to reprint poems or excerpts from their publications.

HarperCollins Publishers, Inc., for "I search among the plain..." from "A Mother's Love" from LIGHT OF THE YEARS by Grace Noll Crowell. Copyright © 1936 by Harper & Row Publishers, Inc. Copyright © renewed 1964 by Grace Noll Crowell. All rights reserved. Reprinted by permission.

Carol Publishing Group for "Every thing in nature..." from A THIRD TREASURY OF KAHLIL GIBRAN edited by Andrew Dib Sherfan. Copyright © 1975, 1973, 1966, 1965 by Philosophical Library, Inc. Published by arrangement with Carol Publishing Group. A Birch Lane Press Book.

PrimaDonna Entertainment Corp. for "My Perfect Mother" by Donna Fargo. Copyright © 1998 by PrimaDonna Entertainment Corp. And for "Thank You, Mother" by Donna Fargo. Copyright © 1996 by PrimaDonna Entertainment Corp. All rights reserved. Reprinted by permission.

Elizabeth Barnett for "I have never met..." by Edna St. Vincent Millay. Excerpt from letter to Cora B. Millay, in Maine, from Edna St. Vincent Millay, in Paris, June 15, 1921. From LETTERS OF EDNA ST. VINCENT MILLAY (Letter 82), Harper & Brothers. Copyright © 1952, 1980 by Norma Millay Ellis. All rights reserved. Reprinted by permission of Elizabeth Barnett, literary executor.

Ayer Company Publishers, Inc. for "The Mother" from ALL IN A LIFETIME by Edgar A. Guest. Copyright © 1970 by Ayer Company Publishers, Inc. All rights reserved.

Amy Cirincione for "Sinusoidal Curve." Copyright © 1999 by Amy Cirincione. All rights reserved. Reprinted by permission.

A careful effort has been made to trace the ownership of poems and excerpts used in this anthology in order to obtain permission to reprint copyrighted materials and give proper credit to the copyright owners. If any error or omission has occurred, it is completely inadvertent, and we would like to make corrections in future editions provided that written notification is made to the publisher:

SPS STUDIOS, INC., P.O. Box 4549, Boulder, Colorado 80306.